The Library of Author Biographies

J. K. Rowling

The Library of Author Biographies

J. K. ROWLING

William Compson

To YG

Published in 2003 by The Rosen Publishing Group, Inc.
29 East 21st Street, New York, NY 10010

First Edition

Library of Congress Cataloging-in-Publication Data

Compson, William.
J. K. Rowling / by William Compson.
    p. cm. — (The library of author biographies)
Summary: Discusses the life, novels, and writing habits of J. K. Rowling, author of the popular "Harry Potter" novels.
Includes bibliographical references (p.) and index.
ISBN 0-8239-3774-7 (library binding)
1. Rowling, J. K. 2. Authors, English—20th century—Biography. 3. Potter, Harry (Fictitious character). 4. Children's stories—Authorship. [1. Rowling, J. K. 2. Authors, English. 3. Women—Biography.]
I. Title. II. Series.
PR6068.O93 Z6 2002
823'.914—dc21

2002006687

Manufactured in the United States of America

This book is neither authorized nor approved by J. K. Rowling.

Table of Contents

Introduction: That's What Friends Are For

Harry Potter is a wizard, and he attends Hogwarts, Britain's top wizard school. But Harry Potter, the hero of J. K. Rowling's Harry Potter novels, is also a schoolboy. He has hopes and fears, feelings and emotions. He gets scared like us; he needs friends just like we do— and just like J. K. Rowling, the writer who brings him to life.

In *Harry Potter and the Chamber of Secrets* (1998), Harry is rescued from the Dursleys (the non-magical, or Muggle, family he lives with) by his best friend, Ron Weasley. Ron and his brothers arrive at the Dursleys' house at 4 Privet Drive in a car. But this is no ordinary car. It's a car that flies.

It's no accident that this old turquoise car should be the one Ron uses to rescue Harry from his life at the Dursleys' house. Neither is it an accident that this car is pictured proudly on the cover of the British edition of the book. When Rowling was seventeen, she was in the "lower sixth" at her high school, Wyedean. (That's the equivalent of eleventh grade.) And she was bored, bored with the small town where she lived—called Tutshill—and bored with school. She dreamed of escaping into great and new adventures. On top of that, she felt like an outsider.

Then a new boy named Séan Harris arrived at school (he, too, felt like an outsider), and the two became great friends. Séan was the first of her friends to get his driver's license (in the United Kingdom, you have to be seventeen to take your driving test), and he had a car—a turquoise Ford Anglia. Rowling has said that, frequently, it's only after she has read what she has written that she notices links between some of the things she writes about and her own experiences. For example, the idea for the car that rescues Harry came from Rowling's friend Séan's car. The vehicle represented freedom from provincial life for Rowling and Harris.

Later on, in *Chamber of Secrets*, Harry and Ron miss the Hogwarts Express (the train that takes them to school), so they put all their stuff back into the car and take off from near King's Cross, the station in London from where the train leaves. They're both scared as they climb higher, but as they get farther from London and up above the clouds, they find their fear replaced by the sheer joy of escaping into a new world.

It's easy to imagine J. K. Rowling and Séan Harris driving along the country lanes near Tutshill, feeling as happy as Harry and Ron— escaping their everyday lives in the old turquoise car. This is one of J. K. Rowling's greatest talents: she can translate feelings into adventures so that you're moved and excited by what her characters are feeling. But she doesn't do it by directly describing her characters' feelings (she says that she has never trusted authors who do that). Instead, she lets her characters' actions describe their feelings for us—whether it's fear, excitement, fun, or danger. And, because of this, we're able to share what Harry, Ron, and their friend Hermione are feeling—feelings that aren't always nice to feel.

Harry's escape from Privet Drive and the feelings of escape in the drive to Hogwarts are just two small examples of what lies at the heart of J. K. Rowling's work. In the Harry Potter novels, time and time again Harry's life is full of difficult decisions about doing what he feels is the right thing and what people think he should do. He is constantly faced with danger and problems, but with the help of his friends and by trusting himself, he manages to figure out the right thing to do. Trust your heart and trust your real friends, J. K. Rowling seems to say, and you will be rewarded. It's an idea that you see not only when you read about Harry Potter but also in J. K. Rowling's life. You can also see this in the dedication in *Harry Potter and the Chamber of Secrets*, which is written for Séan Harris.

It doesn't take long to realize that, as with J. K. Rowling and her old friend Séan, the most important thing about the Harry Potter books is friendship. Harry, Ron, and Hermione are friends, through thick and thin, and it's a friendship that you feel will last well beyond the final book in the Harry Potter series.

1 Beginnings

Joanne Rowling was born on July 31, 1965, in Chipping Sodbury in the south-west of England. (The "K" in her name came later, as we shall see.) Her parents, Peter Rowling and Anne Volant, had met the year before on a train, and it had been love at first sight. Peter was in the Royal Navy, Anne was in the Wrens (Women's Royal Navy Service), and they were both being sent for a posting in Arbroath, Scotland. The train left from King's Cross station in London, and because of this, and as a tribute to her parents, when J. K. Rowling began to write the first Harry Potter book, she immediately thought of King's Cross when she needed a railroad station from which the Hogwarts Express would leave.

However, if you go to King's Cross and look for the barrier that divides platforms nine and ten (as it's mentioned in the Harry Potter books), you won't find it. That's because J. K. Rowling now admits that when she was imagining platforms nine and ten, she was thinking about a different station. She wrote this scene when she was living in Manchester (a city in the north of England), and she confused King's Cross with Euston, another station just up the road from King's Cross.

Rowling's parents were married in London; both were just nineteen years old. But the couple did not want to stay in London, and Peter had found a job in a factory in a part of England known as the West Country. So the couple moved to the small town of Yate, about 100 miles (160 kilometers) from London.

Rowling's first memory is of the day of her sister Dianne's birth at the family home in Yate on June 28, 1967. She says she doesn't remember the actual birth of her sister, but she clearly recalls that her father gave her some Play-Doh to keep her occupied—and she ate it!

In the fall of 1970, at age five, Rowling started school at St. Michael's Church of England School in Winterbourne, a village four miles (six kilometers) from Yate. Just a year later, she wrote her first story. It was called "Rabbit," and it was about a rabbit called Rabbit. She wrote lots of stories about Rabbit and even drew pictures for them. (She now says that they were very boring.) Rowling says that from a very young age, as soon as she was old enough to realize that people actually wrote books (as opposed to books simply magically appearing), she decided that she wanted to be a writer.

In 1974, Peter, Anne, Joanne, and Dianne moved to Tutshill, a small town near the town of Chepstow on the border between Wales and England. Her parents had bought Church Cottage, next door to the village's church and graveyard. Rowling says that her friends thought it was really scary to be living next door to a graveyard but that she and her sister really liked it. In the book *Conversations with J. K. Rowling*, Rowling told the author, Lindsey Fraser, that she is still quite fond of graveyards. In fact, for Rowling, graveyards are a good place to find interesting names—by examining the names of the tombstones. Tutshill is a small place and Church Cottage was just down the road from the village school. Even though it wasn't very far away, Rowling says that she was still always late for school.

It was here that Rowling had her first experience with a nasty teacher, a certain Mrs. Morgan. When she revisited the school as an adult, she told the children that although she really liked coming to school, she was very frightened of Mrs. Morgan. Mrs. Morgan arranged the students' seating in order of their intelligence. On Rowling's first morning, she had a chat with Mrs. Morgan and the students were then given a fractions test. Rowling had never done fractions before and she didn't score well on the test—and so she ended up in what was known as the stupid row.

Later on, Mrs. Morgan moved Rowling to the smart row, but when she did that, Mrs. Morgan moved one of Rowling's friends into the stupid row. Because of the switch, the friend was really angry with Rowling. Rowling now says that Mrs. Morgan was one of the inspirations for Severus Snape, the teacher who is always so nasty to Harry Potter. However, just because Mrs. Morgan wasn't nice to her didn't stop Rowling from returning home and doing what she liked best: writing. It was during this time that Rowling wrote her second story, *The Seven Cursed Diamonds*.

Rowling describes herself at this time as being short, stout, and shy. She wore thick glasses, which were the inspiration for Harry's glasses. She was a bookworm who was often bossy, and she did rather poorly in school. She admits that Harry is able to fly because it is something she would have loved to have been able to do at that time.

Rowling enjoyed living in Tutshill when she was young, but as she moved into her teens, she says things changed. At age eleven, she started at Wyedean Comprehensive (a comprehensive school is the British equivalent of high school), which is in Sedbury, a village two miles from Tutshill. There were some subjects that she never liked and which she admits she wasn't very good at. One of these was metalwork (she made a spoon that was useless); another was woodwork (a badly made photograph frame resulted from this class); and she really didn't like playing sports (she broke her arm playing netball, a game like basketball that is played in British schools by girls).

At most British schools, students wear uniforms, and Rowling was not a fan of the Wyedean uniform, which was yellow and brown—two colors that, to this day, she refuses to wear together. But things weren't all bad at Wyedean. It was there she met her favorite teacher. Miss Shepherd taught English (always the subject Rowling enjoyed the most), and Rowling appreciated her passion for teaching. She says that Miss Shepherd was strict but fair and that this earned her respect. Rowling says that she learned a lot from Miss Shepherd and they still keep in touch with each other.

When *Harry Potter and the Philosopher's Stone* was published in 1997 in the United Kingdom (in the United States it was published in 1998 as *Harry Potter and the Sorcerer's Stone*), Miss Shepherd sent Rowling a letter telling her that she really liked the book. Rowling says that the praise from Miss Shepherd meant more to her than any published review in the press.

As time moved on, Rowling was approaching the next big step in her life. She was going to leave school and go to college. But before that, she had some rather important exams to take.

2 Moving Away

In the Harry Potter books, student wizards study for exams called O.W.L.s, or Ordinary Wizarding Levels. This is another of J. K. Rowling's plays on Muggle ideas transported into the wizarding world. Until 1988, English and Welsh schoolchildren took exams called O-levels or Ordinary levels when they were sixteen. After O-levels come A-levels (or Advanced levels) in which students study three (or sometimes four) subjects for their last two years at school. Because of her interest in language and languages (which you can still detect in the Harry Potter books), Rowling decided to take English, French, and German.

In British schools, a boy or a girl (and sometimes both) are chosen to be headboy or headgirl of the school. Rowling was made headgirl of Wyedean in her last year at the school, a year that ended with her taking her A-levels. But before that, she had to decide which universities she was going to apply to. Her first choice was Oxford—one of Britain's oldest and most prestigious universities—and she took the special exams needed to be considered for a place there. Unfortunately, she was not accepted, so she decided to accept a place she'd been offered at Exeter University, where she eventually decided to go to study French and classics. She now admits that she didn't really want to study French. Rowling says that she is not exactly sure why she chose French at the university other than the fact that it was something that her parents wanted her to do.

Rowling became very interested in politics when her aunt gave her a copy of Jessica Mitford's *Daughters and Rebels* when she was fourteen years old. J. K. Rowling says Jessica Mitford is the writer who was most influential on her career. In fact, Rowling even named her daughter after her. Mitford was a courageous human rights activist who also had a wonderful sense of humor. She was fiercely independent as well as being a passionate socialist who rebelled against her wealthy family—the Mitfords did not think it was necessary for girls to get an education.

Rowling expected the students at Exeter to be interested in politics as well, but on her arrival she was surprised to find that they weren't. During her time at Exeter, she continued to be an avid reader, making the most of the university library. (Among the books she read for the first time at the university were J. R. R. Tolkien's *The Lord of the Rings* [1954–1955], a trilogy that, with its creation of a fantasy world, can be seen to have influenced the Harry Potter novels.) Rowling spent a lot of time at the library, though she wasn't very good at returning books on time.

Rowling admits that she didn't work as hard as she might have done at Exeter— perhaps because as we've seen she didn't really want to study French—but she did enjoy her third year when she went to study in Paris for

Jessica Mitford: Fighting for Her Beliefs

Jessica Mitford was born on September 11, 1917, in Gloucestershire, England. She was one of six daughters born to David Mitford (the Baron of Redesdale) and his wife, Sydney Bowles. The sisters went on to become some of the most scandalous members of the British aristocracy. Nancy Mitford became a novelist and biographer. Diana Mitford married Sir Oswald Mosley, the leader of the British fascist party before World War II, and spent most of the war in jail in London. Another sister, Unity, went to Germany and became a friend of Nazi Germany's dictator, Adolf Hitler, before shooting herself in the head.

J. K. Rowling's heroine, Jessica Mitford, or Decca as she was known—the Mitfords all had nicknames—became a famous civil and human rights campaigner in the United States, but before arriving she had plenty of adventures.

In 1937, Spain was in the middle of a civil war. Jessica heard that her cousin Esmond Romilly had run away from school and was going to fight in the war. She decided to run away with him, but not before charging a camera to her father's account at a big London department store. She was nineteen; Esmond was eighteen and the nephew of Sir Winston Churchill, the famous British politician. When Churchill found out about the couple's elopement, he sent a Royal Navy destroyer to go and pick them up in Bilbao, Spain. Esmond and Jessica then went to North America, where he joined the Royal Canadian Air Force. Sadly, in 1941, at the age of twenty-three, Esmond was killed in a bombing raid over Germany.

Jessica then went to work in Washington, D.C., where she met a young lawyer named Robert Treuhaft. The couple married and moved to Oakland, California, where they joined the American Communist Party. At the beginning of the 1950s, some people were very scared by communists, and committees were set up to find any communists who might be in positions of power. (The main committee was called the House Un-American Activities Committee, or HUAC, and was run by Senator Joseph McCarthy.) Robert and Jessica were called before the committee in the early 1950s but refused to give the names of anyone they knew from the Communist Party.

At this time, Jessica and Robert were researching a book about the American funeral industry. When the book, *The American Way, of Death*, was published in 1963, it became a bestseller and exposed how the funeral industry was overcharging many of its customers. This was just one of many causes the couple fought for. They also supported the civil rights movement (which wanted to give African Americans the same rights and privileges as white people) and the anti–Vietnam War movement. On Jessica Mitford's death from cancer on July 23, 1996, the *New York Times* described her as "a formidable literary figure." Not bad considering she only became an author because, she said, "I figured that the only thing that requires no education and no skills is writing."[1]

a year. It was here that she taught English for the first time, a skill that would become useful to her a few years later.

Rowling completed one more year at Exeter before receiving her degree in 1987 with average grades. She immediately went to London and began a training course to become a bilingual secretary. Looking back, Rowling admits that she would have been a disaster as a secretary. She says that taking the course was even more of a mistake than taking French at Exeter. According to Rowling, when she finished the bilingual secretary program, she just wanted whatever job would provide her with enough money to live and time to write.

That job was with Amnesty International, an organization working to fight human rights abuses. Rowling used her knowledge of French in her work as a research assistant specializing in countries in French-speaking Africa. Like her heroine Jessica Mitford, Rowling was working for worthy causes and fighting for what she believed in.

It was during her time working for Amnesty International that Rowling discovered something that would be helpful later on: she loved writing in cafés. While her colleagues went out to lunch, Rowling would sneak off to cafés to work on the adult novel she was attempting to finish. (She also wrote in cafés to get away from her roommates in the apartment she shared in Clapham Junction, a neighborhood in London.)

Even though she was working for a good cause in a job that gave her the time to keep writing, she wasn't very happy in London. It was time to move on.

3 Harry Turns Up

After three years in London, Rowling decided to move to Manchester—the city where her favorite pop group, The Smiths, came from. Her boyfriend had moved there and she wanted to join him. Rowling says that she doesn't regret the decision to move to Manchester, despite it not being a happy period in her life. It was during a train ride from Manchester to London that her life suddenly changed: Harry Potter arrived. Rowling has talked many times about the moment in June 1990 when the young wizard came to her, but no matter how many times she tells the story, you can feel the excitement she felt that day.

According to Rowling, she was on the train when, all of a sudden, she found herself thinking of the character who would become Harry. She even had a clear mental image of him as a skinny kid. It was an extremely exciting moment for her. She wanted to capture the idea on paper, but after searching through her bag, she realized that she didn't have anything to write with. Then the train was delayed and Rowling could do nothing but patiently wait while all these ideas grew inside her.

By the time she had got off the train and rushed back to Clapham Junction to start writing down her ideas, she had already imagined Ron, Nearly Headless Nick, Hagrid, and Peeves. The emotions she felt in her moment of discovery were, she says, like falling in love: She was scared and excited and happy. She had her idea. Now she just had to write it.

J. K. Rowling says she began by concentrating on the school itself, Hogwarts. It had to be a very orderly and dangerous place. Then she set about finding the right names for her characters. First there was Harry Potter. Rowling's favorite boy's name is Harry—she said if she'd had a son, she'd have called him Harry. "Potter" came from a family who lived next door to the Rowlings in Winterbourne.

According to Rowling, when you're creating a fantasy world, it's really important to have rules. Rowling explained why she felt this way in an interview with Stephen Fry, the English actor and comedian who narrates the British versions of the Harry Potter audiobooks. Rowling says it's best to start out by deciding exactly what your characters can and can't do. However, as a writer, you must be aware that if you give your characters limitless powers, there won't be any reason to have tension or

Language

When asked about where the ideas for her books come from, Rowling has said that it's often not a conscious process—that certain names, for example, come to her without her being aware that they were names she already knew. For example, Rowling didn't recall where "Hogwarts" (the name of the school in the Harry Potter books) came from until a friend reminded her that, seven years earlier, they'd seen lilies in Kew Gardens—the Royal Botanical Gardens in London—that were named Hogwarts.

You can have a lot of fun reading the Harry Potter novels by looking more carefully at the names of places, characters, and spells, because they often give hints of the characters' real personalities. Some are so obvious that you don't notice them at first. (Think of Salazar Slytherin, the founder of Slytherin House, who took the snake as his symbol. What do snakes do? They slither.) Other names require a little more thought or even some research, and a good place to start is *Brewer's Dictionary of Phrase and Fable*.

First published in 1870, the book is full of names of mythical creatures, legendary heroes and villains, and thousands of odd facts and names. Rowling admits that *Brewster's Dictionary of Phrase and Fable* has been a great help to her when coming up with characters' names. One example is the name of superstar author Gilderoy Lockhart. Rowling was thumbing through the *Dictionary of Phrase and Fable* when she found an entry for Gilderoy, a good-looking Scottish highwayman. This was exactly what she was looking for as a first name—it seemed just right. Rowling came across the name Lockhart on a war memorial to World War I. Together, the two names seemed like a perfect fit for how Rowling imagined the character.

Here's a selection of some names and their meanings (for a complete list, go to Rudolf Hein's Website, http://www.rudihein.de/hpewords.htm, titled "Do You Know Mundungus Fletcher?").

Draco Malfoy: Draco is Latin for "dragon" or "giant serpent," and Malfoy means "bad faith" in French (mal = bad; foi = faith).

Minerva McDonagall: Minerva was the Roman goddess of wisdom.

Professor Lupin: This is one of Rowling's favorite characters. Lupin's name gives a hint of his secret. Lupus in Latin means "wolf"; this gives us the word "lupine" in English, which means characteristic of or resembling a wolf.

Lord Voldemort: You-know-who's name (as the magic world calls him) literally means "theft of death" in French.

Sirius Black: Harry's godfather is an Animagus who changes into a dog; in astronomy, Sirius is known as the Dog Star because it's the brightest star in the constellation Canis Major. Canis means "dog" in Latin.

Fawkes: The phoenix who saves Harry at the end of *Chamber of Secrets* is named after Guy Fawkes, one of the participants in the Gunpowder Plot of November 5, 1605. The aim of the plot was to blow up the British Houses of Parliament and the king at the time, James I, as a way of restoring Roman Catholicism as the nation's official religion. The discovery of the plot is still celebrated every November 5 in Britain when effigies of Fawkes (called "Guys") are burned on bonfires and fireworks are set off.

Argus Filch: Argus was a giant who had 100 eyes and was set to guard the goddess Io; filch means "to steal." So Hogwarts's caretaker is perfectly named—he's always on the lookout to steal banned things off students.

drama in your story. And a fantasy story without conflict won't be much of a story.

Accordingly, there are very strict rules for the teenage wizards in the Harry Potter novels. Think of the over 400 items that are banned from the school or how students aren't allowed to use magic in the Muggle world.

But if the magical world is governed by rules meant to make things fair, back in the Muggle world, life is not always so easily controlled.

A couple of days after the idea of Harry came to her, Rowling sat down and wrote the scene in which Harry's parents are killed. Six months later, tragedy struck, and Rowling was forced to live what she'd written about; on December 30, 1990, her mother, Anne, died.

4 To Portugal and Back

Anne Rowling had been diagnosed with multiple sclerosis (MS) ten years earlier. MS is a degenerative disease during which the coatings around nerve cells in the brain and the spinal cord are damaged. This means that a person suffering from MS gradually begins to find it difficult to walk and hold things. Anne had been forced to give up her job helping out in the chemistry lab at Wyedean when her MS began to keep her from holding things without dropping them.

Sufferers also find that their hands and legs often feel numb and they get a pins-and-needles feeling. Slowly, as more and more nerves are damaged, the body finds it difficult to continue carrying out basic functions. Walking, speaking, even breathing become more and more difficult and, eventually, the sufferer finds it hard to control his or her body at all. Anne Rowling had been diagnosed with what is known as the galloping form of the disease, meaning it progresses quickly. It can sometimes take decades for the disease to lead to a sufferer's death; for Anne Rowling, it took just one.

J. K. Rowling is now an ambassador for the Multiple Sclerosis Society of Scotland. She wrote about her mother's suffering with the disease for the newspaper *Scotland on Sunday*. Scotland has the highest rates of MS in the world (scientists don't understand why), but the government's health-care program has one of the lowest budgets in Europe for the one drug, called beta-interferon, that can help MS sufferers.

Rowling says that her mother's death was like "a depth charge" in her life. She had always been very close to her mother—there was only twenty years difference in age between them—and she thought of her as more of an older sister than a mother. Rowling's grief over her mother's death was the inspiration for one of her most touching inventions—the Mirror of Erised in *Harry Potter and the Philosopher's Stone* (*Harry Potter and the Sorcerer's Stone* in North America).

The mirror that Harry stumbles on goes as high as the ceiling and has an inscription around the top that reveals the mirror's special quality: It shows you what you most want to see.

Of course, Harry sees his family, and especially his parents.

What would you see if you looked into the Mirror of Erised? Rowling says she would see her mother. She'd tell her that she has a daughter and she'd describe her. And, of course, she'd tell her mother that she'd written some books that had miraculously become very popular. Rowling says that she'd be chattering for quite some time before she'd realize that she hadn't asked her mother what it was like to be dead. For Rowling, the mirror episode is about realizing that it's not good to dwell on things. Not that you need to forget, but you have to be able to move on.

Rowling was living in Manchester and working at Manchester University at a job she didn't like. She and her boyfriend often argued, but sometimes the arguments provoked creative moments. After one particularly big argument, Rowling checked into the Bourneville Hotel in Manchester and invented Quidditch, the game played in the wizarding world and at which Harry is so good. Rowling had a lot of fun making up the rules for the game, and she still has the notebook she'd written it all down in, diagrams and all. But Rowling was not happy in Manchester, and when her house was burglarized and everything her mother had left her was stolen, she decided it was time to get out.

She had spotted an advertisement in a newspaper about a language school in Oporto (Portugal's second largest city) that needed English teachers. Rowling, who had enjoyed teaching English when she had spent a year in Paris, sent off an application form. After an interview with the school's director, Steve Cassidy, she got the job, and in November 1991, flew out of Manchester to begin her new life. With her, Rowling was carrying all her notes and drafts that were slowly becoming *Harry Potter and the Philosopher's Stone*. In fact, one of the reasons she thought it would be good to go to Portugal was that she would have mornings free to write.

While in Portugal, Rowling taught people of all ages—from eight-year-olds to sixty-two-year-olds—but she says that her favorite age group was teenagers between the ages of fourteen and seventeen because they were excited by life and what it offered them. While at school, she met two fellow teachers who had arrived for the new school year. Jill Prewett and Aine Kiely, who appear in the dedication of *Harry Potter and the Prisoner of Azkaban*, were to help Rowling through some tough times ahead in Oporto.

In March 1992—about five months after her arrival in Oporto—Rowling went out one night and met a journalism student in a bar. When the pair started talking (in English), it turned out that Jorge Arantes had read Jane Austen's novel *Sense and Sensibility*, which Rowling was rereading at the time. (Jane Austen is one of Rowling's favorite authors.) On August 28, 1992, Jorge Arantes asked Rowling to marry him. She said yes, and less then two months later, the couple were married at the Register Office in Oporto. Rowling's sister, Dianne, and her boyfriend, Roger Moore, were there (Moore was a witness) to see Rowling marry

Portugal's Influence on Harry

There seem to be two points where Rowling's time in Portugal plays a part in the Harry Potter novels. The first is more obvious; the second less so. The first is that the founder of Slytherin—one of the four houses at Hogwarts and the one renowned for producing evil wizards—is called Salazar. From 1932 to 1968, Portugal was ruled by a dictator called António de Oliviera Salazar. The second was spotted by Sean Smith in his biography, *J. K. Rowling*, and would seem to be the sort of in-joke that she loves. In *Harry Potter and the Prisoner of Azkaban*, Professor Trelawny tells Lavender Brown that something she wasn't looking forward to was going to take place on October 16—a Friday. The date of Rowling's wedding to her first husband in 1992 was Friday, October 16.

Jorge. Not long afterward, Rowling became pregnant. On July 27, 1993, just four days before her twenty-eighth birthday, she gave birth to a little girl. She called her Jessica, in honor of Jessica Mitford. And, according to

Helping Others

J. K. Rowling is always ready to help causes she holds close to her heart. The first time she helped a charity was in fall 2000 when she gave £500,000 ($785,000) to the National Council for One Parent Families (doubling its budget). The charity works to help parents bringing up children on their own.

In an article she wrote for the charity, she describes not only the terrible time she had when she returned from Portugal but also the way in which one-parent families are seen by society. Just as she returned to the United Kingdom, the then British prime minister, John Major, made a speech that attacked single mothers as being responsible for what he saw as the collapse in society's values. At the time, many politicians were alleging that teenage girls were deliberately getting pregnant so that they would get a free "council flat" (an apartment owned by the local government).

Rowling says that only 3 percent of single parents are teenagers, while 60 percent of single parents who were married are presently divorced, separated, or have been widowed. Along with her donation, she also agreed to be an ambassador for the charity. In her role as ambassador, Rowling helped out by being a public representative for the National Council for One Parent Families. Its goal is to ensure that single parents get the credit and help they deserve.

Rowling, giving birth to Jessica was the best experience of her life.

However, Rowling's moment of happiness was cut short when her relationship with Jorge began to collapse. After one particularly nasty argument, she decided to leave Portugal and return to the United Kingdom with Jessica. She was worried about making money if she stayed in Portugal—she wasn't paid during the language school vacations. Her sister, Dianne, was living in Edinburgh, Scotland, and after visiting her, Rowling decided to stay. She says that perhaps the decision came to her because of her Scottish roots.

When Rowling arrived in Edinburgh, it began to sink in that while it had been easy to rush off from Portugal, the part that came next

Comic Relief

Rowling's biggest contribution to charity has come not through her simply donating money or offering public support, but from two books she wrote. In 2001, Richard Curtis, who wrote screenplays for *Four Weddings and a Funeral* (1994) and *Notting Hill* (1999), asked Rowling if she'd like to contribute something to Comic Relief. The charity—which is not the same as Comic Relief in the United States—raises money to help "some of the poorest and most vulnerable people in the poorest countries in the world." Rowling agreed and came up with two books: *Quidditch Through the Ages* by Kennilworthy Whisp and *Fantastic Beasts and Where to Find Them* by Newt Scamander.

Both books are mentioned in the Harry Potter novels. *Quidditch*—published by Whizz Hard Books—is the book Hermione reads in *Philosopher's Stone*. *Fantastic Beasts* (from Obscurus Books) is on the first year reading list at Hogwarts.

Rowling has said that she really enjoyed writing the books—and it shows. The books are playful, clever, and fun, and there are a lot more jokes than in the novels. Many of these jokes are very British, especially in *Quidditch*. For example, Kevin and Karl Broadmoor are the best-known players for the Falmouth Falcons, a Quidditch team known for its hard play. Broadmoor is also the name of one of the UK's most high-security prisons and psychiatric hospitals, which is found on Dartmoor, a national park not that far from Exeter. There are also references in two Quidditch team names to towns that are important to Rowling: The Wimbourne Wasps, named after Wimbourne in Dorset where her grandparents lived; and the Tutshill Tornados, after the town where Rowling spent her teenage years.

The version of *Fantastic Beasts and Where to Find Them* is a reproduction of Harry's copy (it's full of scribblings, doodles, and comments by Harry, Ron, and Hermione). The creatures detailed in the book are, as in the novels, a mixture of beasts that Rowling has invented (such as the Plimpy, a roundish fish with long legs and webbed feet) and creatures from mythology, such as the Phoenix. And just in case you might have thought that Harry Potter's adventures were seen by their creator as fairy tales, Rowling adds a footnote to the entry on fairies that makes it clear that fairies—and the sentimental way humans portray them—are far from her thoughts when she writes the Harry Potter books.

Muggles have a great weakness for fairies, which feature in a variety of tales written for their children. These "fairy tales" involve winged beings with distinct personalities and the ability to converse with humans (though often in a nauseatingly sentimental fashion). Fairies, as envisaged by the Muggles, inhabit tiny dwellings fashioned out of flower petals, hollowed-out toadstools, and similar objects in nature. They are often depicted as carrying wands. Of all magical beasts, the fairy might be said to have received the best Muggle press.

was not so easy: finding what she was going to do to support herself and her daughter.

In an essay written for the National Council for One Parent Families, Rowling described her feelings on her return. She said that she wasn't able to focus on the reality of the situation until after she had arrived in Edinburgh. It was a few days before Christmas in 1993, and Rowling all of a sudden realized that she would be living on the equivalent of

$109 a week. She describes how collecting her welfare checks from the post office felt terribly humiliating. She worked for two hours a week—she couldn't earn more than £15 ($24) a week or she would lose some of her welfare. As she couldn't pay for child care, she couldn't get a full-time job, but as she had no job, she couldn't pay for child care for Jessica. Rowling was stuck. But there was still Harry, whose adventures were slowly progressing.

It is from this period of her life that the legend of Rowling—the single mother living on next to no money in an unheated apartment and writing in cafés—has sprung. Jessica was still a baby and that meant the only times Rowling could write was when her daughter was sleeping. She had to make the most of her time. Rowling would go for walks with her daughter in a stroller to tire Jessica out. As soon as Jessica was asleep, Rowling would rush into the nearest café to write as much Harry as she could. Looking back now, Rowling says that it's amazing how much you can get done when you have a limited amount of time to work with. Rowling claims that this was her most productive time in terms of words per hour.

One of her favorite places to write was in a café called Nicolson's, which was co-owned by Dianne's husband, Roger Moore. (The two were married just before Rowling came back from Portugal.) Rowling says that the staff there were very friendly to her and she promised to give the café lots of publicity if the books were ever published (a promise she has kept!).

After Rowling became famous, there were many stories spread about her life at this time, and she now says that only about 50 percent of them are true. She told the British Broadcasting Corporation (BBC) that stories about her having an unheated apartment were wrong; not because she wasn't poor but because she's not stupid enough to rent an unheated apartment in Edinburgh in the middle of winter. She also didn't write on napkins because she was too poor to afford paper; she wrote in notebooks. Rowling always writes with a pen and paper, preferably in black ink on "narrow feint," a type of lined writing paper. She types up the books later on.

Yet, as always, Rowling managed to use some of this darkest period of her life to help her with Harry Potter, as you can read in *Harry Potter and the Prisoner of Azkaban*. In Azkaban, the prison of the wizarding world, the guards are the ghastly Dementors. They are the most horrible creatures in the magical world and they make everyone they go near feel as if there is no possible hope or happiness.

During this period, Rowling was feeling very depressed and eventually spent nine months visiting a counselor to help her stop feeling so awful. She told the BBC that the Dementors were a way of showing depression through characters. Go near a Dementor and you will feel as you do when you're completely depressed. When people are depressed, they often find it very difficult to see anything positive in their lives; it feels as if there is no hope left, which is just how the Dementors leave you feeling.

Toward the end of 1994, Rowling decided that she would like to return to teaching. But in Scotland, she needed a special qualification to become a schoolteacher, and to get it she had to go back to the university. She went to a day-long interview for the course and was accepted in January 1995.

Slowly but surely, with the first book nearing completion, J. K. Rowling was putting her life back together.

5 Being Published

Rowling was scheduled to begin her course in August 1995 at Moray House in Edinburgh. But just as it looked like things were finally going her way, she hit another snag. There were supposed to be day-care facilities for students with small children, but unfortunately they had closed. Rowling phoned a few private nurseries, and they said that three terms worth of child care was going to cost between £3,500 and £5,000 (between $5,495 and $7,850). Rowling was desperate; she had to take the course to start earning enough money to get her and Jessica out of their situation, but she simply couldn't afford it. Luckily, a friend came to the rescue and lent her some money.

Finally, she could start her course. It turned out to be what Rowling now describes as the most difficult year of her life in terms of working hard and being under a lot of stress. But in spring 1996, the manuscript was ready, and Rowling went to the library to look in a reference book containing the names and addresses of literary agents and publishers.

She chose one agent and one publisher and sent off the finished manuscript with a cover letter. It was rejected. One reason was that the manuscript she was sending was around 90,000 words and children's novels are usually only about 40,000. But Rowling wasn't discouraged. She picked another agent from the book: Christopher Little. (She liked his name.) Rowling wrote Mr. Little and asked if he would be interested in reading her manuscript. She sent along a few sample chapters and briefly explained what the children's book was about.

He read it, loved it, and agreed to become her agent. (When she met Christopher Little for the first time, he told her that she shouldn't expect to make any money from writing children's books!) After many of the biggest publishers in London had turned down the book, Bloomsbury, a small publishing company that was just starting up a children's book department, agreed to buy the book for £1,500 ($2,355). When this happened, Rowling was completely overwhelmed. It was an amazing thing to realize that she was actually going to be published.

But before her manuscript was published, there was one last thing to do: The publishers asked her to change her name. Rowling was so grateful that they were publishing her book, she would have called herself nearly any name they'd suggested. When she first asked why, she says that the publishers said that just two initials—instead of her name—would look more striking on the book cover. But Rowling didn't think that was the real reason. When she confronted them and suggested that they wanted to hide the fact that she was a female writer, the publishers would only say that they thought boys would really like her book. (Experience has shown publishers that boys supposedly don't like reading books written by women.) As Joanne was her only given name, she chose another to add to her initials—Kathleen, the name of her favorite grandmother, who had died of a heart attack at age fifty-two. This is how Joanne Rowling became J. K. Rowling.

On June 26, 1997, almost exactly a year after she had first sent her sample chapters to Christopher Little, *Harry Potter and the Philosopher's Stone* was published in the United Kingdom. The day it was published, the newly named J. K. Rowling went straight to a bookshop on Prince's Street, the main shopping street in Edinburgh. She was very excited. Her life's ambition had been fulfilled— she was a serious author in a serious bookshop on the shelves with all the other serious authors. In fact, she was so excited that she wanted to take copies off the shelves and sign them before putting them back. (She decided that she might get into trouble with the bookstore if she did, though!)

By this time, Rowling had gained her teaching certificate with a top grade and had been awarded an £8,000 ($12,560) grant by the Scottish Arts Council, an organization that gives money to writers who live in Scotland. With her grant money, she bought a computer (she had typed *Philosopher's Stone* on a manual typewriter). Then one night three months after the publication of the book in the United Kingdom, Christopher Little telephoned her. He was in New York and the rights for the book were being auctioned for the United States. He told her that the auction was going very well, and that the bidding had actually reached five figures. Of course, this news was a shock for Rowling. An hour later, they were at six figures! When Rowling's U.S. editor, Arthur Levine, called her, he told her not to panic.

Harry Potter and the Philosopher's Stone had been sold for $105,000, a virtually unheard of amount for a children's book, especially a first novel by an unknown writer. This moment was Rowling's first brush with fame and the publicity that goes with it—an experience she has had to get used to, but will never accept. The British press loved the story of the poor, single mother who had sold her first book for so much money. In fact, it seemed as though every article that mentioned Harry Potter discussed the fact that Rowling was a divorced, single parent who was struggling financially. Rowling says that she felt as though she had a large tattoo on her head proclaiming her single, divorced, and penniless status.

However, for Rowling, the next stage wasn't how to spend her newly earned money, but how to finish the second book in the series. She admits that the big advance for *Philosopher's Stone* was such a shock that for the first time in her life she got writer's block. Looking back, she now says that although the second book was incredibly hard to finish— like the *Goblet of Fire*, which was also very difficult to write—it is her favorite book. The manuscript for *Harry Potter and the Chamber of Secrets* was delivered to her publishers on time, but Rowling still wasn't happy with it and asked to have it back for six weeks of fine-tuning.

The book was published in the United Kingdom in 1998 to great reviews—it almost immediately went to the top of the best-seller list. At the same time, *Harry Potter and the Philosopher's Stone* was being published in the United States, except that it was now called *Harry Potter and the Sorcerer's Stone*. Rowling was happy to change things—she knew that after such a big advance, she and Arthur Levine, her U.S. editor at Scholastic (a large children's publishing company in New York), had to make the book as successful with American children as possible. The title, which Rowling herself suggested, was not the only difference, and she estimates that there are around 200 small changes between the two versions. Most are simply words that mean different things in British English and

Reviews of *Harry Potter and the Sorcerer's Stone*

"Though all this hocus-pocus is delightful, the magic in the book is not the real magic of the book. Much like Roald Dahl, J. K. Rowling has a gift for keeping the emotions, fears and triumphs of her characters on a human scale, even when the supernatural is popping out all over . . . On the whole, *Harry Potter and the Sorcerer's Stone* is as funny, moving and impressive as the story behind its writing. J. K. Rowling, a teacher by training, was a 30-year-old single mother living on welfare in a cold one-bedroom flat in Edinburgh when she began writing it in longhand during her baby daughter's nap times. But like Harry Potter, she has wizardry inside, and has soared beyond her modest Muggle surroundings to achieve something quite special."[1] —Michael Winerip, *New York Times*, February 14, 1999

"The hero of J. K. Rowling's *Harry Potter and the Sorcerer's Stone* is an outsider, one who, like many other outsiders in kids' literature, learns to value the things that have always made him feel separate from the people around him, and who also learns that the means of escape from his solitary existence has been within him all along. The book is a dream of belonging, and of discovering self-sufficiency and courage. What matters, though, is the flesh Rowling puts on those thematic bones. I don't think you can read 100 pages of *Harry Potter and the Sorcerer's Stone* before you start feeling that unmistakable shiver that tells you you're reading a classic."[2] —Charles Taylor, salon.com, March 31, 1999

American English, such as "jumper," which in British English means "sweater." One change that Rowling didn't like was the change of Mum to Mom, so that stayed as is.

Harry Potter and the Sorcerer's Stone may have entered the best-seller list at number 135, but things quickly changed. The book shot up the lists, and by the time *Chamber of Secrets* was published in the United Kingdom in 1998, there were already enough fans that the U.S.

Reviews of *Harry Potter and the Chamber of Secrets*

"The mystery, zany humor, sense of a traditional British school (albeit with its share of ghosts, including Moaning Myrtle who haunts the girls' bathroom), student rivalry, and eccentric faculty, all surrounded by the magical foundation so necessary in good fantasy, are as expertly crafted here as in the first book. Fans who have been thirsting for this sequel will definitely not feel any disappointment. In fact, once they have read it, they will be lusting for the next."[3]—Sally Estes, *Booklist*, May 15, 1999

"As she did in Harry Potter and the Sorcerer's Stone, Rowling delivers plenty of ghoulish giggles, including a 'deathday' party for a 500-year-old ghost, peevish poltergeists, exploding wands and magic potions aplenty. And in young Potter . . . she has created a hero as resourceful, brave and loyal as Luke Skywalker himself."[4] — Cathy Hainer, *USA Today*, December 28, 2000

publisher, Scholastic, was beginning to get worried. Desperate fans who couldn't wait for the American edition to come out in October 1999 simply went online to get a copy from British Web sites. Scholastic—which had paid a lot of money for the rights to publish the book in the United States—was forced to move forward the publication date not only for *Chamber of Secrets* (which eventually came out in June 1999) but also for the third book in the series.

Harry Potter and the Prisoner of Azkaban was published in October 1999. Suddenly, Rowling realized that she was becoming something of a celebrity. A tour to promote

It's Not Just Voldemort

"These types of writings are nothing more than Satan's way to undermine the family."[5]

Voldemort isn't Harry's only enemy. To some religious groups, the Harry Potter novels are neither fun nor exciting—they're dangerous. "The only people that can logically see Harry Potter books as harmless fiction are the same people that believe the DEVIL HIMSELF is only harmless fiction,"[6] says one Web site.

What worries these groups is that in the novels witches and wizards are presented as good people, when according to their religious beliefs, witches and wizards are representatives of Satan. One site says that Harry's lightning-shaped scar is a Satanic "S."[7] And some say that reading Harry Potter books will make children interested in becoming witches and wizards themselves.

In Alamogordo, New Mexico, Pastor Jack Brock of the Christ Community Church went so far as to organize a book burning during which copies of the Harry Potter novels were thrown into a bonfire.

J. K. Rowling says that she is neither a witch nor does she believe in magic. She says that people who want to stop children from reading Harry Potter novels are underestimating children's capacity to see what is fact and what is fantasy. Rowling responds to these charges by noting that she isn't aware of any instances where her books have led children to a belief in the supernatural.

the book began in Boston, and when Rowling approached the store, she was stunned at what she saw. There was, she says, a gigantic line that went around two blocks. She had to be snuck in the back entrance, and when she appeared, she was met by a huge scream from all the waiting children. Rowling compared the experience to that of being a rock star. At the end of that day in Boston, she had signed 1,400 copies of her books. Not long afterward, Rowling had the top three books on the *New York Times* best-sellers list.

When *Philosopher's Stone* (or *Sorcerer's Stone*) was published, it received good reviews both in the United Kingdom and in North

America. But, as it is with many books, it wasn't the newspapers or television that spread the news of Harry Potter's arrival: It was people telling other people about this great book they'd read. Harry Potter's fame spread—like it does in the book's wizarding world—by word of mouth.

6 J. K. Superstar

Potter Four, as the fourth book became known in the publishing world, took a long time to write. Rowling says that it was easily the most difficult book she has written, and for the first time, she missed her deadline. The cause of the two-month delay? After she had written half of the book, Rowling realized that there was a problem with the plot. It didn't work. (This is really important to J. K. Rowling; she says she hates books with holes in their plots.) Because of this, she had to start again, and in the process she wrote out a character, a cousin of Harry's best friend, Ron Weasley.

This character was supposed to play the same role that the journalist Rita Skeeter now plays in the book, as a "conduit for information outside the school."[1] Then there was chapter 9, "The Dark Mark." During an online chat with Comic Relief in the United Kingdom, Rowling admitted that this chapter nearly drove her mad. She rewrote it thirteen times and was so frustrated that she thought of leaving it out and simply putting in a page stating that because chapter nine was too difficult to write, readers should skip it and go straight to chapter 10. And, of course, there was the expectation—and the pressure that came with it—that had built since the success of *Azkaban*.

To avoid the problems that had occurred with *Chamber* and *Azkaban*, it was announced that Potter Four would be released at midnight on July 8, 2000, on both sides of the Atlantic. However, there remained one big secret still to be revealed. In interviews she gave after the publication of *Azkaban*, Rowling refused to

Reviews of *Harry Potter and the Prisoner of Azkaban*

"The beauty here lies in the genius of Rowling's plotting. Seemingly minor details established in books one and two unfold to take on unforeseen significance, and the finale, while not airtight in its internal logic, is utterly thrilling. Rowling's wit never flags, whether constructing the workings of the wizard world (just how would a magician be made to stay behind bars?) or tossing off quick jokes (a grandmother wears a hat decorated with a stuffed vulture; the divination classroom looks like a tawdry tea shop). The Potter spell is holding strong."[2] —*Publishers Weekly*

"Though Rowling is undoubtedly a fine storyteller, her books are underpinned by a conservative sense of what storytelling can achieve. Look closer at this comic, gothic world where pictures speak and every panel may hide a secret tunnel, and you find a classic boarding school fantasy, complete with dodgy food, sadistic teachers, bullies and unshakable loyalties.[3] —Claire Armistead, *The Guardian* (London), July 8, 1999 give the title of Potter Four, saying that she was superstitious about titles. But, when the book was finally released, Rowling revealed that the real reason was far simpler: She just couldn't decide what to call it. Her working title was *Harry Potter and the Doomspell Tournament*. Then she changed it to *Harry Potter and the Triwizard Tournament*, before finally settling on *Harry Potter and the Goblet of Fire*. This title was leaked to a British newspaper about ten days before it was published, ruining the surprise.

Finally, at midnight on July 8, *Harry Potter and the Goblet of Fire* was released to the reading public—all 734 pages in the United States and 636 in the United Kingdom. Children in both countries lined up for hours to get their copies. The publishers were ready and had printed millions of copies of the book. In the United Kingdom alone, Bloomsbury printed 1,027,000 copies of the book; normally in the United Kingdom about 20,000 copies of popular children's books are printed. In the United States, Scholastic printed 5.3 million copies; normally it's around 100,000.

Later that morning in London, Rowling arrived at King's Cross station in a turquoise Ford Anglia. Waiting for her was a crowd of screaming children (and their parents), a mass of photographers and journalists, and a train platform renumbered 93/4 for the morning. Bloomsbury, the British publisher, had come up with the idea of publicizing the book by hiring a steam train (normally named the Queen of Scots), renaming it the Hogwarts Express (the train that takes pupils to Hogwarts in the novels), and touring the country to promote the book. At 11 AM (the time that the Hogwarts Express leaves in the books) and after facing the photographers, J. K. Rowling climbed aboard the train and it drew out of King's Cross, the station she has always considered to be romantic.

Unfortunately, the romance of a steam engine shooting through the English countryside didn't last very long. Soon after leaving the station, the train's fifty-seven-year-old steam engine developed a problem, and the Hogwarts Express had to be towed by a diesel engine.

After touring the United Kingdom (the train finished its journey in Perth, Scotland), Rowling set off for stage two of the *Goblet of Fire* tour: North America. On the Canadian leg of the tour, Rowling revealed that she had once nearly visited the country. Her father had been offered a job in Canada when she was eight years old. Sadly, it fell through, leaving her very disappointed. However, Rowling could hardly have been disappointed at the turnout for her only public reading in Toronto.

The organizers decided to hold the reading not in a bookstore or even a theater, but at the SkyDome—the stadium where the Toronto Blue Jays play baseball. Tickets cost from CAN $5.85 ($3.69) to as high as CAN $234 ($148), and more than 16,000 children and adults turned up to hear J. K. Rowling read for thirty minutes from chapter 4 of *Goblet of Fire*.

Rowling admits that the noise of the crowd was so loud that she had to wear earplugs. After she had finished, she took the earplugs out to hear the crowd and she says that it took her breath away! J. K. Rowling had become a superstar. While Rowling doesn't deny that she has made a

Harry's Return

"Harry is the kid most children feel themselves to be, adrift in a world of unimaginative and often unpleasant adults—Muggles, Rowling calls them—who neither understand them or care to. Harry is, in fact, a male Cinderella, waiting for someone to invite him to the ball. In Potter 1 [*Sorcerer's Stone*], his invitation comes first by owl (in the magic world of J. K. Rowling, owls deliver the mail) and then by Sorting Hat; in the current volume it comes from the Goblet of Fire, smoldering and shedding glamorous sparks."[4] —Stephen King, *The New York Times*, July 23, 2000

lot of money from the Harry Potter books, she says that she had no idea what she was getting herself into. She says that she wonders if she would have been better suited to being just a moderately successful author.

Not long after *Philosopher's Stone* was published, Hollywood became interested in

Harry. But to begin with, Rowling and her agent, Christopher Little, weren't very interested in Hollywood. One reason was that Rowling was determined to make sure that a film would remain true to her book. That didn't just mean that a film should not change the story but also that it should remain as British as her books. Rowling didn't want Hogwarts moved to a secluded spot in, say, Montana. Harry Potter must remain British.

The first producer to express an interest in making a film of *Harry Potter and the Philosopher's Stone* was David Heyman, a British producer who had just moved back to London from Los Angeles. He first approached Christopher Little in the spring of 1997. It took a long time (and it meant beating out many other companies), but at the end of 1999, David Heyman and the Hollywood studio Warner Bros. got a deal: They paid $1 million for the rights to the first three books.

During the time that the deal had taken to put together, Harry Potter had become a big name. Hence, a big name was needed to direct it. Steven Spielberg and Rowling talked about his directing the film, but he dropped out.

Rowling was very protective of her characters and her invented world. She believes he wouldn't have been content not to have been able to let his imagination take over.

On March 28, 2000, it was announced that a director had been chosen: Chris Columbus, the director of the movies *Mrs. Doubtfire* and *Stepmom*. The next day, Columbus flew to London and with David Heyman took a train from King's Cross to visit Rowling. They talked for four hours, Columbus bombarding Rowling with questions about Harry Potter and the world of Hogwarts.

As part of the deal signed with Warner Bros., Rowling had final approval of the finished script, meaning that she could say no if she didn't like it. She was very relieved when she first met Steve Kloves, the screenwriter chosen to adapt the novel to the screen. Rowling says that the first time she met him, he asked her to guess who his favorite character was, and Rowling was certain he would name Ron Weasley, because he's so easy to love. But when Kloves replied that he preferred Hermione, Rowling was thrilled. Kloves's response indicated to Rowling—who always admits that Hermione is based on herself as a child—that Steve was the right man for the job.

The last thing to sort out was probably the most difficult: Who would be Harry? The filmmakers searched for a year, looked at over 40,000 children, and were beginning to get desperate. Then luck stepped in. David Heyman and Steve Kloves were at the theater in London and there he was, sitting with his father: the boy who would be Harry. It turned out that David Heyman knew the boy's father and a week later his son was asked to audition.

It took two months, but finally it was decided: Daniel Radcliffe was going to be Harry Potter. "I was in the bath at the time, and my dad came running in and said, 'Guess who they want to play Harry Potter?'" Radcliffe told *Premiere* magazine. "And I started to cry. It was probably the best moment of my life."[5] Columbus and Rowling both agreed that Radcliffe was the Harry they'd been looking for. And just in case they weren't certain that they'd made the right choice, there was one uncanny coincidence. Daniel Radcliffe's birthday is July 31—the same day as both Harry and Rowling!

Radcliffe had starred in a BBC production of Charles Dickens's *David Copperfield* and in a single feature film. The actors chosen to play Ron (Rupert Grint) and Hermione (Emma Watson) had never acted on camera before, but the rest of the cast were all veterans of stage and screen. And most important to Rowling, they were all British.

During the film's production, Columbus and the film's crew were anxious to make a film as close to Rowling's imagined world as they could, and she worked closely with them to help. She drew a map of Hogwarts for the production designer, Stuart Craig; she told Columbus exactly how an invisibility cloak should look (among many other things); she told Alan Rickman, who plays Severus Snape, all about his character's history; and she told Robbie Coltrane, who plays Hagrid, that he should imagine the Hogwarts groundskeeper as a large Hell's Angel biker who seems kind of intimidating, but when he gets off his motorcyle, he surprises you by talking about his garden and his pretty flowers.

Still concerned for her creations even after having worked so hard with the filmmakers, Rowling admitted that she became increasingly frightened as the viewing approached. And when she actually sat down to watch the film, she was terrified. Yet at the premiere of the film in London on November 4, 2001, Rowling was all smiles as she arrived with her boyfriend, Dr. Neil Murray. (They were married on December 26, 2001, in Scotland.) She liked the film; all her hard work had paid off, and she had the film she'd imagined.

Rowling has always said that she planned to write seven Harry Potter books—one for every year Harry is at Hogwarts. And sitting in a safe somewhere in the United Kingdom is the ending of the seventh book. It has already been written, and it's in a yellow paper folder. She wrote the ending as a way of showing herself that one day she would get to the end; one day she would wrap the whole story up; one day Harry Potter would have no more adventures at Hogwarts.

After book seven, Harry Potter will leave the school he loves so much and start a life outside the walls of Hogwarts. When that happens, millions of disappointed fans will have to come to terms with there being no more Harry Potter, but there's one person who will probably miss him more than anyone else. When the time comes, Joanne Rowling—the woman who has been thinking of Harry, dreaming of him, writing about him, living with him since 1990—will, like her character, have to leave the world she created and go forward into the next great adventure.

What's J. K. Reading?

As an author, J. K. Rowling always tells children who are thinking of being writers that reading is the basis for writing. So what did J. K. Rowling read as a child and what does she read now?

Children's Books

The Little White Horse by Elizabeth Goudge was Rowling's favorite book as a child. Her mother gave her a copy of Elizabeth Goudge's 1946 novel when she was eight years old. The two authors share a passion for finding suitable names for their characters (Goudge has Maria Merryweather, Miss Heliotrope, and Wiggins as her central characters), but there is one particular aspect of Goudge's style that J. K. Rowling particularly appreciates. Goudge always describes the food her characters are eating—a detail Rowling uses in the Harry Potter books.

She also loved Paul Gallico's *Manxmouse*, C. S. Lewis's *Chronicles of Narnia*, Clement Freud's *Grimble*, and Kenneth Grahame's *The Wind in the Willows*. She has particularly fond memories of Grahame's book because she remembers her father reading it to her when she was sick with the measles.

Adult Novels

J. K. Rowling's all-time favorite author is Jane Austen (1775–1817). She has lost count of the number of times she has read Austen's novel *Emma*. Her favorite living writer is the Irish novelist Roddy Doyle, who she calls a genius.

She says that the two authors have a surprisingly similar way of creating characters and that both have one very important talent: they're funny.

She also says that she enjoys Vladimir Nabokov, a writer as interested in playing with language as J. K. Rowling, as well as the French author Colette. And don't forget Jessica Mitford (see pp. 22–24), who Rowling describes as the writer who influenced her the most.

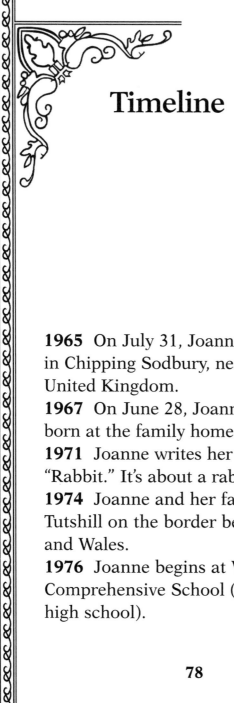

Timeline

1965 On July 31, Joanne Rowling is born in Chipping Sodbury, near Bristol, in the United Kingdom.

1967 On June 28, Joanne's sister, Diane, is born at the family home in Yate.

1971 Joanne writes her first story, called "Rabbit." It's about a rabbit called Rabbit.

1974 Joanne and her family move to Tutshill on the border between England and Wales.

1976 Joanne begins at Wyedean Comprehensive School (the equivalent of high school).

1980 Joanne's mother, Anne, is diagnosed with multiple sclerosis.

1983 After taking her A-level exams, Joanne leaves school and, in September, takes a place at Exeter University in the southwest of England studying French and classics.

1985 Joanne spends a year working in Paris as a teacher as part of her university course.

1987 Joanne graduates from Exeter University and goes to London. She finds a job working with the human rights campaign group Amnesty International.

1990 On a delayed train ride from Manchester to London, Joanne first has the idea for Harry Potter.

Joanne's mother, Anne, dies from multiple sclerosis.

1991 After seeing an advertisement in the local newspaper, Joanne takes a job teaching English in Oporto, Portugal.

1992 In March, she meets a Portuguese journalism student, Jorge Arantes, and on October 16 the couple are married.

1993 On July 27, Joanne gives birth to a daughter whom she names Jessica, after her heroine, Jessica Mitford.

In October, Joanne leaves her husband in Portugal and moves back to Edinburgh, Scotland, with Jessica.

1994 Joanne and Jessica live in a small apartment in Edinburgh. Joanne spends every spare minute writing the first Harry Potter book.

1995 Joanne sends two sample chapters of *Harry Potter and the Philosopher's Stone* to a literary agent in London. The agent, Christopher Little, agrees to represent her. She agrees to change her name to J. K. Rowling— the K standing for Kathleen, the name of her favorite grandmother.

Joanne divorces her husband.

1996 Joanne qualifies as a teacher and begins a job at Leith Academy.

1997 *Harry Potter and the Philosopher's Stone* is published in the United Kingdom.

In September, the book is sold to U.S. publisher, Scholastic; the title is changed to *Harry Potter and the Sorcerer's Stone*.

1998 *Harry Potter and the Chamber of Secrets* is published in the United Kingdom and the United States.

1999 *Harry Potter and the Prisoner of Azkaban* is published in the United Kingdom in the spring and in the fall in the United States.

Warner Bros. buy the rights to turn the Harry Potter books into a series of movies. The studio picks Chris Columbus to direct them.

2000 *Harry Potter and the Goblet of Fire* is published at the same time in the United Kingdom and the United States.

2001 *Harry Potter and the Philosopher's Stone* (*Sorcerer's Stone* in the United States) is released onto screens across the world.

J. K. Rowling marries Dr. Neil Murray.

2002 J. K. Rowling writes two small books— *Quidditch Through the Ages* and *Fantastic Beasts and Where to Find Them*—for the British charity, Comic Relief. For each copy sold, the charity receives £2 ($3).

Selected Reviews from *School Library Journal*

Harry Potter and the Sorcerer's Stone
October 1998

Gr 4–7—Harry Potter has spent eleven long years living with his aunt, uncle, and cousin, surely the vilest household in children's literature since the family Roald Dahl created for *Matilda* (Viking, 1988). But like Matilda, Harry is a very special child; in fact, he is the only surviving member of a powerful magical family. His parents were killed by the evil Voldemort, who then mysteriously vanished, and the boy grew up completely ignorant of his own powers, until he received notification of his acceptance at the Hogwarts School of Witchcraft and Wizardry. Once there, Harry's life changes dramatically. Hogwarts is exactly like a traditional British boarding school, except that the professors are all wizards and witches, ghosts roam the halls, and the surrounding woods are inhabited by unicorns and centaurs. There he makes good friends and terrible enemies. However, evil is lurking at the very heart of Hogwarts, and Harry and his friends must finally face the malevolent and powerful Voldemort, who is intent on taking over the world. The delight of this book lies in the juxtaposition of the world of Muggles (ordinary humans) with the world of magic. A whole host of unique characters inhabits this world, from the absentminded Head Wizard Dumbledore to the sly and supercilious student Draco Malfoy to the loyal but not too bright Hagrid. Harry himself is the perfect confused and unassuming hero, whom trouble follows like a wizard's familiar. After reading this entrancing fantasy, readers will be convinced that they, too, could take the train to Hogwarts School, if only they could find

Platform Nine and Three Quarters at the King's Cross Station. —Eva Mitnick, Los Angeles Public Library, California

Harry Potter and the Chamber of Secrets
July 1999

Gr 3–8—Fans of the phenomenally popular *Harry Potter and the Sorcerer's Stone* (Scholastic, 1998) won't be disappointed when they rejoin Harry, now on break after finishing his first year at Hogwarts School of Witchcraft and Wizardry. Reluctantly spending the summer with the Dursleys, his mean relatives who fear and detest magic, Harry is soon whisked away by his friends Ron, Fred, and George Weasley, who appear at his window in a flying Ford Anglia to take him away to enjoy the rest of the holidays with their very wizardly family. Things don't go as well, though, when the school term begins. Someone, or something, is (literally) petrifying Hogwarts' residents one by one and leaving threatening messages referring to a Chamber of Secrets and an heir of Slytherin. Somehow, Harry is often around when the attacks happen and he is soon suspected of being the perpetrator. The climax has Harry looking very much like Indiana Jones, battling a giant serpent in the depths of the awesome and terrible Chamber of Secrets. Along with most of the teachers and students introduced in the previous book, Draco Malfoy has returned for his second year and is more despicable than ever. The novel is marked throughout by the same sly and sophisticated humor found in the first book, along with inventive, new, matter-of-fact uses of magic that will once again have readers longing to emulate Harry and his wizard friends. —Susan L. Rogers, Chestnut Hill Academy, Pennsylvania

Harry Potter and the Prisoner of Azkaban
October 1999

Gr 4–8—Isn't it reassuring that some things just get better and better? Harry is back and in fine form in the third installment of his adventures at Hogwarts School of Witchcraft and Wizardry. His summer with the hideous Dursley family is cut short when, during a fit of quite understandable rage, he turns his Aunt Marge into an enormous balloon and then runs away. Soon, it becomes quite apparent that someone is trying to kill him; even after Harry is ensconced in the safety of fall term at Hogwarts, the attacks continue. Myriad subplots involving a new teacher with a secret, Hermione's strangely heavy class schedule, and enmity between Ron's old rat, Scabbers, and Hermione's new cat, Crookshanks, all mesh to create a stunning climax. The pace is non-stop, with thrilling games of Quidditch, terrifying Omens of Death, some skillful time travel, and lots of slimy Slytherins sneaking about causing trouble. This is a fabulously entertaining read that will have Harry Potter fans cheering for more. —Eva Mitnick, Los Angeles Public Library, California

Harry Potter and the Goblet of Fire
August 2000

Gr 4 Up—Harry is now fourteen years old and in his fourth year at the Hogwarts School of Witchcraft and Wizardry, where big changes are afoot. This year, instead of the usual Inter-House Quidditch Cup, a Triwizard Tournament will be held, during which three champions, one from each of three schools of wizardry (Hogwarts, Durmstrang, and Beaux-batons), must complete three challenging magical tasks. The competitors must be at least seventeen years old, but the Goblet of Fire that determines the champions mysteriously produces Harry's name, so he becomes an unwilling fourth contestant. Meanwhile, it is obvious to the boys' allies that the evil Voldemort will use the Tournament to get at Harry. This hefty volume is brimming with all of the imagination, humor, and suspense that characterized the first books. So many characters, both new and familiar, are so busily scheming, spying, studying, worrying, fulminating, and suffering from unrequited first love that it is a wonder that Rowling can keep track, much less control, of all the plot lines. She does, though, balancing humor, malevolence, school-day tedium, and shocking revelations with the aplomb of a circus performer. The Triwizard Tournament itself is a bit of a letdown, since Harry is able, with a little help from his friends and even enemies, to perform the tasks easily. This fourth installment, with its deaths, a sinister ending, and an older and more shaken protagonist, surely marks the beginning of a very exciting and serious battle between the forces of light and dark, and Harry's fans will be right there with him. —Eva Mitnick, Los Angeles Public Library, California

Selected reviews from *School Library Journal* reproduced with permission from *School Library Journal*. Copyright © 1999, 2000 by Cahners Business Information, a division of Reed Elsevier, Inc.

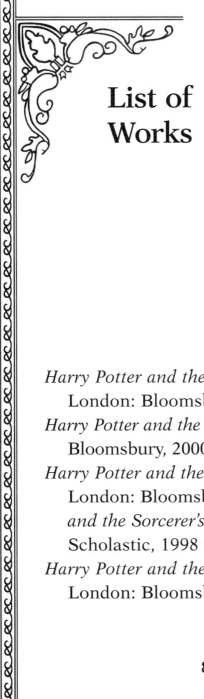

List of Works

Harry Potter and the Chamber of Secrets.
   London: Bloomsbury, 1998.
Harry Potter and the Goblet of Fire. London:
   Bloomsbury, 2000.
Harry Potter and the Philosopher's Stone.
   London: Bloomsbury, 1997/*Harry Potter
   and the Sorcerer's Stone*. New York,
   Scholastic, 1998 (U.S. title).
Harry Potter and the Prisoner of Azkaban.
   London: Bloomsbury, 1999.

Scamander, Newt. *Fantastic Beasts and Where to Find Them*. London: Bloomsbury, 2001. Whisp, Kennilworthy, *Quidditch Through the Ages*. London: Bloomsbury, 2001.

List of Awards

Harry Potter and the Chamber of Secrets
The Booksellers Association/The Bookseller
    Author of the Year (1998)
British Book Awards, 1998 Children's Book
    of the Year
The Federation of Children's Books Group
    (FCBG) Children's Book Award 1998,
    Overall winner and Longer Novel Category
Nestlé Smarties Book Prize 1998, Gold
    Medal 9–11 years
North East Book Award (1999)

North East Scotland Book Award (1998)
Scottish Arts Council Children's Book Award
  (1999)
Whitaker's Platinum Book Award (2001)

Harry Potter and the Goblet of Fire
Children's Book Award, 9–11 category (2001)
The Hugo Award (2001)
Scottish Arts Council Book Award (2001)
Whitaker's Platinum Book Award (2001)

**Harry Potter and the Philosopher's Stone/
Harry Potter and the Sorcerer's Stone**
Birmingham Cable Children's Book
  Award (1997)
British Book Awards, 1997 Children's Book of
  the Year
FCBG Children's Book Award 1997, Overall
  winner and Longer Novel Category
Nestlé Smarties Book Prize (1997), Gold Medal
  9–11 years
Sheffield Children's Book Award (1998)
Whitaker's Platinum Book Award (2001)
Young Telegraph Paperback of the Year (1998)

Harry Potter and the Prisoner of Azkaban
The Booksellers Association/The Bookseller
  Author of the Year (1998)
British Book Awards, 1999 Author of the Year

FCBG Children's Book Award 1999, Longer
    Novel Category
Nestlé Smarties Book Prize 1999, Gold Medal
    9–11 years
Whitaker's Platinum Book Award (2001)
Whitbread Children's Book of the Year (1999)

Glossary

aristocracy A segment of society made up of people who have inherited noble titles; the word is often applied to people who think that they make up the highest or most important part of society.

communism A political system that centralizes power in a government. Communist parties ruled the Soviet Union from 1917 until 1991 and countries in Eastern Europe from 1945 to 1991.

conduit A way of sending something; for example, you can have a conduit of information.

degenerative A disease that slowly destroys the body by attacking tissues or organs until they do not work properly or at all.

effigy A crude representation of a person (a portrait or a statue) that is shown in public—and often burned or hanged—as a way of protesting against that person.

elopement When a couple secretly runs away and gets married.

fascist A right-wing political movement that celebrates the idea of a country's importance and power. When in power, fascist governments are usually run by a dictator who crushes any opposition to the government with force; fascist governments held power in various countries in Europe from the 1920s through the 1970s.

headboy/headgirl A male/female student who is selected to be the pupils' representative to the teachers.

literary agent A person who represents an author and who negotiates with publishers on an author's behalf when contracts are being discussed.

National Health The name given to the British system of free health care funded by taxes.

occult Usually written as "the occult"; having to do with supernatural powers or knowing about them.

perennial Something that is always present or is always happening.

scandalous Offensive or shocking.

For More Information

Web Sites

Due to the changing nature of Internet links, the Rosen Publishing Group, Inc., has developed an online list of Web sites related to the subject of this book. This site is updated regularly. Please use this link to access the list:

http://www.rosenlinks.com/lab/jkro/

For Further Reading

Colbert, David. *The Magical Worlds of Harry Potter.* London: Puffin, 2001.

Fraser, Lindsey. *Conversations with J. K. Rowling.* New York: Scholastic, 2001.

Goudge, Elizabeth. *The Little White Horse.* Oxford: Lion, 2000.

Lewis, C. S. *The Chronicles of Narnia.* New York: HarperCollins, 1996.

Smith, Sean. *J. K. Rowling: A Biography.* London: Michael O'Mara, 2001.

Bibliography

Amazon.com. "Magic, Mystery, and Mayhem." Retrieved February 26, 2002 (http://www.amazon.com/exec/obidos/ts/feature/6230/002-4718948-8838459).

Armistead, Claire. "Wizard, but with a Touch of Tom Brown." *The Guardian*, July 8, 1999. Retrieved March 2, 2002 (http://www.guardian.co.uk/Archive/Article/0,4273,3881430,00.html).

Bettelheim, Bruno. *The Uses of Enchantment.* London: Penguin, 1988.

Brewer's Dictionary of Phrase and Fable, revised by Adrian Room. London: Cassell, 1999.

British Broadcasting Corporation. *J. K. Rowling: Harry Potter and Me.* December 28, 2001.

Canadian Broadcasting Corporation. "This Morning." Retrieved February 21, 2002 (http://www.cbc.ca/programs/thismorning/sites/books.rowling_001023.html).

Christian Resources Net. *"Harry Potter and the Sorcerer's Stone*: It's JUST fantasy!" Retrieved February 21, 2002 (http://www.daveandangel.com/CRN/Harry_Potter_and_The_Sorcerers_Stone_Just Fantasy.html).

Christian Resources Net. "J. K. Rowling Harry Potter and Witchcraft." Retrieved February 21, 2002 (http://www.daveandangel.com/CRN/Harry_Potter_and_Witchcraft.html).

Colbert, David. *The Magical Worlds of Harry Potter.* London: Puffin, 2001.

Comicrelief.com. "Harry's Books." Retrieved March 14, 2002 (http://www.comicrelief.com/harrysbooks/pages/transcript.shtml).

Cowell, Alan. "All Aboard the Potter Express."

New York Times, July 10, 2000. Retrieved March 12, 2002 (http://www.nytimes.com/library/books/071000rowling-interview.html).

exposingsatanism.org. "Harry Potter: A New Twist to Witchcraft." Retrieved February 21, 2002 (http://www.exposingsatanism.org/harrypotter.htm).

Fraser, Lindsey. *Conversations with J. K. Rowling*. New York: Scholastic, 2001.

Fry, Stephen. Bloomsbury.com. "Interview with J. K. Rowling." Retrieved March 4, 2002 (http://www.bloomsburymagazine.com/harrypotter/muggles/ram/q1.ram).

Goudge, Elizabeth. *The Little White Horse*. Oxford: Lion, 2000.

Hainer, Cathy. "Second Time's Still a Charm." *USA Today*, December 28, 2000 (http://www.usatoday.com/life/enter/books/book112.htm).

Hattenstone, Simon. "Harry, Jessie, and Me." *The Guardian*. August 8, 2001. Retrieved February 20, 2002 (http://www.guardianunlimited.co.uk/Archive/Article/0,4273,4037903,00.html).

Heine, Rudolf. "Do You Know Mundungus Fletcher?" Retrieved January 10, 2002 (http://www.rudihein.de/hpewords.htm).

King, Stephen. "Wild About Harry." *The New York Times*, July 23, 2000. Retrieved March 3, 2002 (http://query.nytimes.com/search/fullpage?res=9406E0D91F38F930A15754C0A9669C8B63).

Lewis, C. S. *The Magician's Nephew*; *The Lion, the Witch and the Wardrobe*; *The Horse and His Boy*. London: Collins, 2001.

Renton, Jennie. "The Story Behind the Potter Legend." *Sydney Morning Herald*, October 29, 2001. Retrieved March 10, 2002 (http://www.smh.com.au/news/0110/29/entertainment/entertain1.html).

Richards, Linda. "J. K. Rowling: A Profile." *January*, October 2000. Retrieved February 22, 2002 (http://www.januarymagazine.com/profiles/jkrowling.html).

Rowling, J. K. *Harry Potter and the Chamber of Secrets*. London: Bloomsbury, 1998.

Rowling, J. K. *Harry Potter and the Goblet of Fire*. London: Bloomsbury, 2000.

Rowling, J. K. *Harry Potter and the Philosopher's Stone.* London: Bloomsbury, 1997.

Rowling, J. K. *Harry Potter and the Prisoner of Azkaban.* London: Bloomsbury, 1999.

Rowling, J. K. "J. K. Rowling Feature." Retrieved February 28, 2002 (http://www.ncopf.org.uk/page/scripts/index.php?section=News&page=JK+Rowling+Feature).

Scamander, Newt. *Fantastic Beasts and Where to Find Them.* London: Bloomsbury, 2001.

scholastic.com. Transcript of J. K. Rowling's Live Interview on Scholastic.com. February 3, 2000. Retrieved March 4, 2002 (http://www.scholastic.com/harrypotter/author/transcript1.htm; http://www.scholastic.com/harrypotter/author/transcript2.htm).

Seaton, Matt. "If I Could Talk to My Mum Again I'd Tell Her I Had a Daughter—and I Wrote Some Books and Guess What Happened?" *The Guardian*, April 18, 2001. Retrieved March 4, 2002 (http://www.guardianunlimited.co.uk/Archive/Article/0,4273,4171517,00.html).

Smith, Sean. *J. K. Rowling: A Biography.* London: Michael O'Mara, 2001.

Taylor, Charles. "This Sorcery Isn't Just for Kids." Salon.com, March 31, 1999. Retrieved March 3, 2002 (http://www.salon.com/mwt/feature/1999/03/cov_31featurea.html).

Weir, Margaret. "Of Magic and Single Motherhood." Salon.com, March 31, 1999. Retrieved March 3, 2002 (http://www.salon.com/mwt/feature/1999/03/cov_31featureb.html).

Whisp, Kennilworthy. *Quidditch Through the Ages.* London: Bloomsbury, 2001.

Winerip, Michael. "Children's Books." *The New York Times*, February 14, 1999. Retrieved February 24, 2002 (http://query.nytimes.com/search/full-page?res=9406E4D61F38F937A25751 C0A96F95826).

Source Notes

Chapter 2

1. Jessica Mitford, *The New York Times*, July 24, 1996.

Chapter 5

1. Michael Winerip, *The New York Times*, February 14, 1999.
2. Charles Taylor, salon.com, March 31, 1999.
3. Sally Estes, *Booklist*, May 15, 1999.
4. Cathy Hainer, *USA Today*, December 28, 2000.
5. http://www.exposingsatanism.org/ harrypotter.htm.
6. Christian Resources Net, *"Harry Potter and the Sorcerer's Stone*: It's JUST fantasy!" (www.daveandangel.com/CRN/ Harry_Potter_and_The_Sorcerers_Stone_ Just_Fantasy.html).

7. Christian Resources Net, "J. K. Rowling Harry Potter and Witchcraft" (www.daveandangel.com/CRN/Harry_Potter_and_Witchcraft.html).

Chapter 6

1. Jeff Jensen, "'Fire' Storm," *Entertainment Weekly* on ew.com (www.ew.com/ew/report/0,6115,85523~5~~,00.html).
2. *Publisher's Weekly*, as featured on www.bn.com (http://shop.barnesandnoble.com).
3. Claire Armistead, "Wizard, but with a Touch of Tom Brown," *The Guardian*, July 8, 1999 (www.guardian.co.uk/Archive/Article/0,4273,3881430,00.html).
4. Stephen King, *The New York Times*, July 23, 2000.
5. Sean M. Smith, "We're Off the See the Wizards," *Premiere*, November 2001, p. 106.

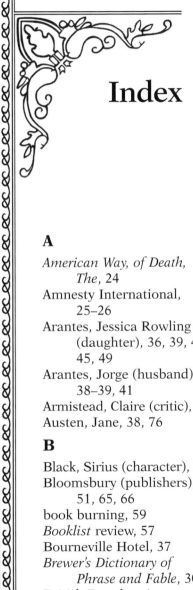

Index

About the Author
William Compson, like J. K. Rowling, is from the West Country in southwest England.

Photo Credits
Cover, p. 2 © AP/Wide World Photos.

Series Design and Layout
Tahara Hasan

Editor
Annie Sommers